The
FOOLISH
DICTIONARY

GIDEON WURDZ.

The

FOOLISH DICTIONARY

An exhausting work of reference
to un-certain English words, their
origin, meaning, legitimate
and illegitimate use,
confused by

A FEW PICTURES

Executed by

GIDEON WURDZ

Master of Pholly, Doctor of Loquacious
Lunacy, Fellow of the Royal
Gibe Society, etc., etc.

THE ROBINSON, LUCE
COMPANY, BOSTON
MDCCCCIV

PRYOR PUBLICATIONS
WHITSTABLE AND WALSALL

Specialist in Facsimile Reproductions

Member of
Independent Publishers Guild

75 Dargate Road, Yorkletts, Whitstable,
Kent CT5 3AE, England
Tel. & Fax: (01227) 274655
E-mail: alan@pryor-publications.co.uk
www.pryor-publications.co.uk

Kent Exporter of the Year Awards Winner 1998/2000

Every effort has been made to trace copyright ownership

ISBN 0 946014 35 3

A full list of Titles sent free on request

To

MY DOG,

Who first heard these lines

And didn't run away

MAD,

I Reverently Dedicate

This Tome.

" A Fool may give a Wise Man counsel."

P r e f a c e .

In this age of the arduous pursuit of peace, prosperity and pleasure, the smallest contribution to the gaiety, if not to the wisdom, of nations can scarcely be unwelcome. With this in mind, the author has prepared "The Foolish Dictionary," not in serious emulation of the worthier—and wordier—works of Webster and Worcester, but rather in the playful spirit of the parodist, who would gladly direct the faint rays from his flickering candle of fun to the shrine of their great memories.

With half a million English words to choose from, modesty has been the watchword, and the author has confined himself to the treatment of only about half a thousand. How wise, flippant, sober or stupid, this treatment has been, it is for the reader alone to judge. However, if from epigram, derivative or pure absurdity, there be born a single laugh between the lids, the laborer will accredit himself worthy of his hire.

In further explanation it should be said that some slight deference has been made to other wits, and the definitions include a few quotations from the great minds of the past and present. As for the rest, the jury will please acknowledge a plea of guilty from

GIDEON WURDZ.

ABBREVIATIONS.

Bet. . . . . . . Between.

Dist. . . . . . . Distinguish.

Eng. . . . . . . English.

Fr. . . . . . . French.

Ger. . . . . . . German.

Grk. . . . . . . Greek.

Lat. . . . . . . Latin.

Syn. . . . . . . Synonym.

v. i. . . . . . . Verb intransitive.

v. t. . . . . . . Verb transitive.

It's a long lane that has no ashbarrel.

Distilled waters run deep.

ABSINTHE From two Latin words, *ad*, and *sinistrum*, meaning "to the bad." If in doubt, try one. (Old adage, "Absinthe makes the jag last longer.)

ABSTINENCE

From the Persian *ab*, water, and *stein*, or tankard. Hence, water-tankard, or "water wagon."

ACCESSION A beheading process by which you may either win or lose a political job. Old spelling, *Axe-session*.

ACCIDENT A condition of affairs in which presence of mind is good, but absence of body better.

ADAMANT From "Adam's Aunt," reputed to be a hard character. Hence, anything tough, or hard.

ADORE From *add*, annex, and *ore*, meaning wealth. Example, foreign nobles who marry American heiresses *adore* them.

ADVICE A commodity peddled by your lawyer and given away by your mother-in-law, but impossible to dispose of yourself. Famous as the one thing which it is " More blessed to give than receive." **GOOD ADVICE** Something old men give young men when they can no longer give them a bad example.

ADVERSITY A bottomless lake, surrounded by near-sighted friends.

AFFINITY Complimentary term for your husband or your wife. Sometimes a synonym for "Your finish."

AFTERTHOUGHT A tardy sense of prudence that prompts one to try to shut his mouth about the time he has put his foot in it.

AGE Something to brag about in your wine-cellar and forget in a birth-day book. The boast of an old vintage, the bug a boo of an old maid.

ALCOHOL A liquid good for preserving almost everything except secrets.

ALDERMAN

A political office known as the Crook's Road to Wealth. From Eng. *all,* and Greek *derma*, meaning skin—"all skin."

ALIMONY An expensive soothing syrup, prescribed by the judge for a divorcee's bleeding heart. (Old spelling, *allay money*).

ALLOPATHY From Eng. *all*, everybody, and Grk. *pathos*, pain. Pain for everybody. **HOMEOPATHY** From Grk. *homoios*, same, and *pathos*. Pain, just the same.

ALPHABET A toy for the children found in books, blocks, pictures and vermicelli soup. Contains 26 letters and only three syllables.

ANCESTORS The originators of the Family Tree, a remarkable sex paradox in which the Ann sisters are always the four fathers.

ANGEL A heavenly ineligible, with wings and a harp; or, an earthly eligible, with money and a heart.

ANTE-ROOMS Euphemistic term for Canfield's, New York City.

ANTE-IMPERIALIST A patriot whose conscience works overtime.

ANTIMONY A metallic substance discovered by Valentine in 1450, and now extensively used in the arts — particularly poker.

APPENDICITIS A modern pain, costing about $200 more than the old-fashioned stomach-ache.

ARGUMENT Breaking and entering the ear, assault and battery on the brain and disturbing the peace.

ARSON Derived from the Hebrew. (See INSURANCE).

ARTIST Commonly, the individual long haired and short-suited, having a positive pose and an uncertain income. Often shy on meal-tickets but strong on technique and the price of tripe sandwiches. An artist may be a barber, a boot-black, a Sargent or a Paderewski.

ATHLETE

A dignified bunch of muscles, unable to split the wood or sift the ashes.

AUGUR One who bored the ancients with prophecies.

AUTOMOBILE

From Eng. *ought to,* and Lat. *moveo,* to move. A vehicle which ought to move, but frequently can't.

AUTOMOBILIST A land lubber on wheels made up to resemble a deep sea diver.

Fine feathers make fine feather-beds.

A stitch in time saves embarrassing exposure.

BABY
From Grk. *babai*, wonderful. Parents are yet to be heard from who don't think theirs is a " wonder."

A noctural animal to which everyone in a sleeping-car is eager to give a wide berth.

BACHELOR From Latin *baculus*, a stick, unattached. Hence, an unattached man, which any lady may stick, stick to, or get stuck on.

BACKBITER A mosquito.

BALANCE Something wanted by book-keepers and often lost by topers. May be found in a cash-book or the kangaroo gait.

BANDIT An outlaw. See ALDERMAN.

BARBER A brilliant conversationalist, who occasionally shaves and cuts hair. Syn. for Phonograph.

BARS Things found in harbors, hotels, fences, prisons, courts and music. (Those found in courts and in music are full of beats),

BARGAIN

 A disease common to women, caught in the Sunday papers and developed in department stores on Mondays. Symptoms, loud talk, pushing and shoving, a combination prize-fight and football scrimmage. (Old spelling *Bark-gain*).

BASEBALL A game in which the young man who bravely strikes out for himself receives no praise for it.

BAT Senior partner of Bat, Ball & Co., and never found without the rest of the firm, as it takes several high-balls to make one short bat.

BEACH A strip of sand, skirted by water; covered with lady-killers in summer, life-savers in winter, and used as a haven — or heaven — for Smacks the year around.

BENEDICT A married male.

BENEDICTINE A married female.

BENEDICTION Their children.

BERTH An aid to sleep, invented by Pullman. Lower preferred.

BIRTH An aid to life, discovered by Woman. Higher preferred.

BICYCLE-SKIRT A abbreviated garment that makes women look shorter and men longer.

BIGAMY A form of insanity in which a man insists on paying three board bills instead of two.

BILLIOUSNESS A liver complaint often mistaken for piety.

BILL-OF-FARE A list of eatables. Distinguished from Menu by figures in the right-hand column.

BIOGRAPH A stereopticon picture taken with a chill and shown with tremors.

BIRDIE A term a woman is apt to apply to a man she is playing for a jay.

BIRTHDAY Anniversary of one's birth. Observed only by men and children.

BLUBBER The useful product of a dead whale. The useless product of a live baby.

BLUE The only color we can feel. **INVISIBLE BLUE** A policeman.

BLUSH A temporary erythema and calorific effulgence of the physiognomy, aeteologized by the perceptiveness of the sensorium, in a predicament of inequilibrity, from a sense of shame, anger or other cause, eventuating in a paresis of the vase-motorial, muscular filaments of the facial capillaries, whereby, being divested of their elasticity, they become suffused with a radiance emanating from an intimidated praecordia.

BOARD An implement for administering corporal punishment, used by mothers and landladies. "The Festive Board" may be a shingle, a hair-brush a fish-hash breakfast or a stewed prune supper.

BOHEMIA (Not on the map.) A land flowing with canned milk and distilled honey and untroubled by consistency, convention, conscience or cash. A land to which many are called and few chosen.

BONE One Dollar — the original price of a wife. Note, Adam, who had to give up one bone before he got Eve.

BONNETS A female head trouble, which is contracted the latter part of Lent and breaks out on Easter.

BOODLE Money, born of poor, but dishonest parents, and taken in by the Graft family.

BORROW v. t., to swap hot air for cold coin.

BOWER A shady retreat, in general.

BOWERY A shady retreat in New York.

BRACE Security for the trousers.

BRACER Security for the stomach.

BRACELET Security for the pawn-broker.

BRAIN The top-floor apartment in the Human Block, known as the Cranium, and kept by the Sarah Sisters — Sarah Brum and Sarah Bellum, assisted by Medulla Oblongata. All three are nervous, but are always confined to their cells. The Brain is done in gray and white, and furnished with light and heat, hot or cold water, (if desired), with regular connections to the outside world by way of the Spinal Circuit. Usually occupied by the Intellect Bros., — Thoughts and Ideas — as an Intelligent Office, but sometimes sub-let to Jag, Hang-Over & Co.

BRAND Something carried on the hip, by either beast or man. Can be found on the outside of a short, red steer, or the inside of a long, black bottle.

BRASS BAND A clever though somewhat complicated arrangement for holding a crowd together.

BRICK An admirable person made of the right sort of clay and possessing plenty of sand. What your friends call you before you go to the wall — but never afterward.

BRIMSTONE A little bit of Hades, which finds its match on earth and smells to heaven. Better to strike it here than in the hereafter.

BREVITY A desirable quality in the Fourth of July oration but not in the fireworks.

BROKE A word expressing the ultimate condition of one who is too much bent on speculating.

BUM   A fallen tough.

BUMP   A tough fall.

BUNCO   The art of disseminating knowledge in the rural districts.

BY-STANDER   One who is injured in a street fight.

People who live in glass houses should dress in
the dark.

Don't put all your eggs in one basket — try an
incubator.

AB Affair for a drive.

CABBY Driver for a fare.

CACHINNATION

 The hysterical ''Ha-Ha.'' Syn. for Carrie Nation.

CADDIE A small boy, employed at a liberal stipend to lose balls for others and find them for himself.

CAFE A place where the public pays the proprietor for the privilege of tipping the waiters for something to eat.

CAJOLE v. t., From Grk. *kalos,* beautiful, and Eng. *jolly,* to jolly beautifully.

CALCIUM An earthly light that brightens even the stars.

CANNIBAL A heathen hobo who never works, but lives on other people.

CAPTIVATE From Lat. *caput,* head, and Eng. *vacate,* or empty, — to empty the head. Note, Women who have captivated men.

CÁPE A neck in the sea.

CAPER A foot in the air.

CARNEGIE-ITIS

 A mania for burning money. Contracted in a Pennsylvania blast furnace, developed in a Scotch castle and now epidemic in American public libraries.

CART v. t., To take off.

CARTOON The take-off.

CAULIFLOWER A Cabbage with a college education.

CAVALRY That arm of the military service that engages in the real hoss-tilities.

CEMETERY The one place where princes and paupers, porters and presidents are finally on the dead level.

CHAMPAGNE The stuff that makes the world go round.

CHAIR Four-legged aid to the injured.

CHARITY Forehanded aid to the indigent

CHAUFFEUR A man who is smart enough to operate an automobile, but clever enough not to own one.

CHRISTIAN A member of any orthodox church.

CHRISTMAS A widely observed holiday on which the past nor the future is of so much interest as the present.

CHUMP Any one whose opinion differs radically from ours.

CIGARETTE A weed whose smoke, some say, should never be inhaled, and still more insist should never be exhaled.

CINDER One of the first things to catch your eye in travelling.

CIVILIZATION An upward growth or tendency that has enabled mankind to develop the college yell from what was once only a feeble war-whoop.

COLLECTOR A man whom few care to see but many ask to call again.

COLLEGE From Fr. *colle*, pasted or stuck, and *etude*, study. A place where everyone is stuck on study. (?)

COLONEL

A male resident of Kentucky.

See KERNEL.

COMPLIMENT v. t., From Eng. *con,* — hot air, and Lat. *pleo,* to fill. Hence, to fill with hot air.

COMPLEXION Color for the face. From Eng. *complex,* difficult, and *shun,* to avoid. To avoid difficulty, buy it of the druggist.

COMMENDATION From Eng. *con,* a josh, and *mend,* to fix up. Hence, a fixed-up josh.

CONDUCTOR From Eng. *coin,* and Lat. *duco,* to command. One who commands the coin.

CONSCIENCE The fear of being found out.

COOK A charitable institution, providing food and shelter for Policemen.

CORPS A big bunch of fighters. (Dist. bet. cores found in apples and corps found in arms).

CORSET From Fr. *corps,* shape, and *sec,* rough. Rough on the shape.

COSMETIC A new face-maker. From Grk. *kosmos,* order, and Eng. *medic,* or doctor,— ordered by the doctor. (See Complexion.)

COT A snooze for one.

COTILLON A dance for eight.

CREDIT Something for nothing.

CREDITOR Something with nothing.

CREDULITY A feminine virtue and a masculine vice.

CREMATION A means of disposing of the dead likely to become very popular, especially with women who are so fond of having the last retort.

CRITIC A wet blanket that soaks everything it touches.

CROOK One who exceeds the speed limit in Law & Order Ave. A Misfit in the Straight and Narrow Way.

CROW A bird that never complains without caws.

CULTURE A degree of mental development that produces tailor made women, fantastically-sheared poodles and dock-tailed horses.

CUPID A driver of sharp darts.

CUPIDITY A driver of sharp deals.

CYNIC A man who knows the price of everything and the value of nothing.

All work and no play makes Jack A Dead One.

Out of fight, out of coin. — *The Pugilist's Plaint.*

ABBLE v. t., To play in water.

DABBLE IN STOCKS — Same thing.

DACHSHUND A low-down dog.

DANCE A brisk, physical exercise, invented by St. Vitus.

DATES A fruit commonly plucked from the Family Tree and spread on the leaves of history. (Dist. bet. Dates and Peaches, which are often associated.)

DEAD Without life. See Boston.

DEADER Pompeii.

DEADEST Philadelphia.

DEADBEAT One who makes a soft living by sponging it.

DEBT A big word beginning with Owe, which grows bigger the more it is contracted.

DEE-LIGHTED

An Oyster Bay localism, derived from delighted.

(Patent and Dramatic rights to this word are, until March 4, 1905, the exclusive property of T. Roosevelt, Esq., Subsequent editions of The Foolish Dictionary will define the word at length.)

DELEGATE From Eng. *dally,* to loaf, and Fr. *gate*, spoiled. A spoiled loafer. For **WALKING DELEGATE,** see Sam Parks, Sing Sing, N. Y.

DEMAGOGUE From Grk. *demos*, people, and Eng. *gag*. One who gags the people.

DEMOCRACY A mysterious country, bounded on the east by Richard Olney, on the west by Willie Bryan, on the north by Dave Hill and on the south by Bennie Pitchfork Tillman.

DEN A cavity.

DENT To punch.

DENTIST One who punches the face and fills cavities.

DEUCE An honest card, in fact the only one that is never known to beat tray.

DEVIL

An old rascal mentioned in the Bible, now reported engaged to Mary McLane.

DIAMOND A bright gem the sparkle of which sometimes renders a woman stone-blind to the defects of the man proffering it.

DIARY An honest autobiography. A good keep sake, but a bad give-away.

DIGNITY A narrow, unstable bearing which mental spindle-shanks try to stand upon when they have no other support.

DICKENS An author; polite term for the devil.

DIE An effect.

DIET Frequently a cause.

DIMPLE A ripple in the gentle whirlpool of a pretty woman's smile.

DIPLOMAT An international liar, with an elastic conscience and a rubber neck.

DISCOUNT Something often sold in place of goods.

DISCRETION An instinctive preception that enables us to say, "Oh, shut up!" to the small, weak man, and "I beg your pardon, but I do not entirely agree with your views," to the large, strong one.

DIVE A gambler's retreat.

DIVIDENDS A gambler's reward.

DIVORCE Nominally, separation of husband and wife from the bonds of matrimony. In the vicinity of Newport it is frequently a legal formula that immediately precedes a fashionable wedding.

DOCK A place for laying up.

DOCTOR One who lays you up.

DREAM   What a man may call a woman, though a Pill may have suggested it. Sweethearts are dreams because they seldom come true ; wives, because they're often a night-mare, and both because they go by contraries.

DRAFT (DRAUGHT)   What gives a cold, cures a cold, and pays the doctor's bill.

DROP-STITCH   A kind of feminine hosiery designed to prevent the men from paying too much attention to the open-work, "peek-a-boo" shirt-waist.

DRUM   Something noisy, and made to beat.

DRUMMER   Something noisy, but impossible to beat. From the Grk. *drimus,* meaning sharp. Hence, something sharp, that always carries its point and sticks whoever it can.

DUST   Mud with the juice squeezed out.

DYNAMITE

The peroration of an anarchist's argument.

DYSPEPSIA   A good foundation for a bad temper.

Out of sight, only in mind. — *Ballad of the Blind Beggar.*

A word to the wise is useless.

AGLE The national bird of a Christian country; (the United States.) Presumably chosen on account of its being a bird of pray.

EARL A title of nobility.

EARLY A title of stupidity. See old saw,
"Early to bed and early to rise,
Makes a man a farmer!"

EARTH

A solid substance, much desired by the seasick.

ECHO The only thing that can cheat a woman out of the last word.

ECONOMY Denying ourselves a necessary to-day in order to buy a luxury to-morrow.

EGG

A wholesome, yet fowl, product, of no use until broken. Sometimes a cure for indigestion or bad acting.

ELECTION

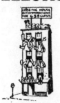 A periodical picnic for the American People. Held in booths, where the Voter puts in his ballot, and The Machine elects whatever it chooses. A day when the lowliest may make their mark and even beggars may ride; when the Glad Mit gets promiscuous and everything is full — particularly the lodging-houses.

ENCORE A greedy theatre-goer's desire to get more than his money's worth. From the Fr. *en,* among, and *cochon,* pig, — common among pigs.

ENGAGEMENT In war, a battle. In love, the salubrious calm that precedes the real hostilities.

ENTHUSIAST One who preaches four times as much as he belives and believes four times as much as a sane man ought to.

EPITAPH A statement that usually lies above about the one who lies beneath.

EQUATOR

 An imaginary line around the earth. Recently held by J. P. Morgan.

ERR To make a mistake.
ERRATIC Full of mistakes.

ETHER One of the world's three great com-
posers — the others being Gas and Chloro-
form — whose airs are popular among the
suffering.

ETIQUETTE A convenient code of conduct
which makes Lying a virtue and Snobbishness
a righteous deed.

EVOLUTION A clever trick performed by one
Darwin, who made a monkey of Adam.

EXCURSION From *ex,* former, and Grk. *kairo,*
to enjoy. Hence, a tiresome journey —
formerly an enjoyment — sold at half price.

EXERCISE Bodily exertion requiring a $10,000
gymnasium, a ten-acre lot and impossible
raiment. Originally confined to the wash-tub
and the wood-pile.

EXPANSION A combination of Grand Larceny
and Piracy, involving the destruction of the
Constitution and Declaration of Independence.
— Boston.
    The benevolent assimilation of previously
oppressed peoples — Washington, D.C.
    A doubtful commercial experiment. — Wall
Street.
    The white man's burden. — Kipling.

EXPLOSION A good chance to begin at the
bottom and work up.

EXPOSITION An overgrown Department Store,
usually opened a year or two behind time.

It's never too late to spend.

A bird on the plate is worth two on the bonnet.

FACE A fertile, open expanse, lying mid-way between collar button and scalp, and full of cheek, chin and chatter. The crop of the male face is hair, harvested daily by a lather, or allowed to run to mutton-chops, spinach or full lace curtains. The female face product is powder, whence the expression, "Shoot off your face." Each is supplied with lamps, snufflers and bread boxes.

FAILURE The quickest method known for making money.

FEINT A pugilist's bluff.

FAINT A woman's bluff.

FAITH A mental accomplishment whereby an ear-ache becomes a Symphony Concert, a broken finger a diamond ring and a "touch" an invitation to dine.

FAKE A false report.

FAKIR A false reporter.

FAME Having a brand of cigars named after you.

FAMILY

 Originally a wife and several children, a matter of pride to the possessor. Now obsolete among the careful, or confined to the wife, a bull pup and a canary bird.

FARE. The cost of a ride. See old adage, "Only the brave can work their fare."

FAULT About the only thing that is often found where it does not exist.

FICTION. The Constitutional fiat that "all men are created equal."

FIDDLER A violinist before he becomes the virtuoso who refuses to play a real tune.

FIRMNESS That admirable quality in ourselves that is detestable stubbornness in others.

FIG Nothing. Note, "I don't care a fig," etc.

FIG LEAF A small outer garment, next to nothing, worn by Adam 4000 B. C. and occasionally revived by Bostonian Art Committees.

FISHING An heroic treatment tried by some laymen to avoid falling asleep in church on Sunday.

FLAT A series of padded cells, commonly found in cities, in which are confined harmless mono maniacs who imagine Home to be a Sardine Box.

FLATTERY Cologne water, to be smelled of but not swallowed.

FLUE An escape for hot air.

FLUENCY The art of releasing the same.

FLUSH From Grk. *phlox*, heat. A rush of color to the cheek, or hand, caused by the bodily- or poker-heat.

FLY A familiar summer boarder who mingles with the cream of society, gets stuck on the butter and leaves his specs behind.

FLY-SCREEN An arrangement for keeping flies in the house.

FOOT The understanding of a girl from the west.

FOOT-PATH Chicago, Ill.

FOOTBALL A clever subterfuge for carrying on prize-fights under the guise of a reputable game.

FOREIGNER

 One who is eligible to the police force. From Grk. *fero,* to carry off, and *enara,* spoils. One who carries off the spoils.

FORBEARANCE The spirit of toleration shown when a man who knows, patiently listens to a fool who does not.

FRANC Twenty cents, in French.

FRANKFURTERS Four for twenty, in German. Derived from *frank,* open, and *fortitude,* meaning brave. Sold in the open and eaten by the brave.

FROST An old flame after the engagement is broken off.

FUN Joy.

FUNCTION Devoid of joy.

As ye sew, so shall ye rip.

Money makes the mayor go.—*Proverbs of Politics.*

ALLON From the Fr. *galonner*, to make tight. Note, one is sufficient.

GALLANTRY This word is now almost obsolete. It was formerly employed to express a deferential attention on the part of the man who in a crowded car gave up his seat to the ladies.

GAMBLER From the Grk. *gumnos*, stripped to the skin. And the gambler's the one that does it.

GARDEN From the Fr. *garantir*, to make good. Hence, a place where lovers make good.

GARLIC From Grk. *gar*, for, and Lat. *liceor*, to bid. Good for the biddies.

GEM A breakfast muffin. With the newly married, syn for "a precious stone."

GERM   A bit of animal life living in water.

GERMAN

 More animal life, living on beer.

GIRAFFE   The champion rubber-neck of the world, and the longest thirst on record.

GLOBE   An all-round proposition which has furnished its shareholders a living for several thousand years, though its stock is two-thirds water.

GOAT   The honored founder and oldest inhabitant of Harlem, N. Y.   Elsewhere, not in good odor.

GOLF   An excuse for carrying unconcealed weapons and a Scotch breath.

GONDOLA   A pleasure craft which plies in Venice, at World's Fairs and other popular watering places.   From Eng. *gone*, and Lat. *dolor*, sadness, or Eng. *dollar*.   Sadness gone; also, a gone dollar.

GORE   Blood.   Shed daily in Chicago abattoirs but never spilled in French duels.

GOSSIP Derived either from the Grk. *gups,* vulture, or Fr. *gosier,* wind-pipe. Hence, a vulture that tears its prey to bits, or an exercise of the wind-pipe from which every victim gets a blow.

GOUT The undesirable scion of High Living, which frequents the lowest joints and is mentioned only in the Invalid's Foot-Notes.

GOWN From Lat. *gaudium,* joy. A thing of beauty and a joy forever; if from Paris, generally an article of some Worth.

GUNPOWDER A black substance much employed in marking the boundry lines of nations.

GUM A substance for sticking.

GUM-GAME A game in which some one is stuck.

GUTTER A school in which we may study the dregs of humanity or read the reflection of the stars.

There's many a slip twixt the toe and the heel.

Where there's a will there's a lawsuit.

AIR-DRESSER A linguist whose posi.on in life enables him to do his head-work with his hands.

HAMMER A small, busy implement carried by blacksmiths, geologists and Knockers for breaking iron, rock or friendship.

HAMMOCK From the Lat. *hamus,* hook, and Grk. *makar,* happy. Happiness on hooks Also, a popular contrivance whereby love-making may be suspended but not stopped during the picnic season.

HAND A much desired possession, supplied by The Damsel or The Dealer. **GLAD HAND.** The beggar's plea, the politician's sceptre and the drummer's ablest assistant.

HANDMAIDEN A manicure.

HARANGUE The tiresome product of a tireless tongue. From Eng. *hear,* and Lat. *angor,* pain. Painful to hear.

HARMONY From the Grk. *arnumi,* strain. Hence, full of strains.

HASH ?

HATCH To develop eggs.

HATCHWAY Place for developing eggs; a hen-coop.

HAY-FEVER A heart trouble caused by falling in love with a grass widow.

HEARSE Seen on the dead.

HEARSAY Heard on the dead.

HEARSE A handsome vehicle in which the man who has always been a tail-ender is finally permitted to lead the procession.

HEART A bloody organ, kept in a trunk, played by beats, and enjoyed only after it is lost or given away.

HEAVE To raise.

HEAVEN A good place to be raised to.

HEDGE A fence.

HEDGEHOG One who hogs the fences. A Bill-Poster.

HELL Poverty.

HEREDITY The cause of all our faults. From Fr. *here,* wretch, and Eng. *ditty,* song. The song of the wretched.

HEROISM

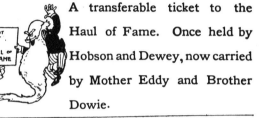

A transferable ticket to the Haul of Fame. Once held by Hobson and Dewey, now carried by Mother Eddy and Brother Dowie.

HIP A popular location for the retail liquor business.

HISTORY The evil that men do.

HIT A chance for first place, first base or first blood.

HOCK v. t., To "soak" what we least need. In Germany, they generally "Hock the Kaiser."

HOMEOPATHY See Allopathy.

HOOT MON! The Scottish National Hymn.

HOP To skip.
HOPPER A skipper.

HOPE A desire for better things to come that makes a grass widow willing to try it again. Also, a draft on futurity, sometimes honored, but generally extended.

HORN A sharp point.

HORNET Still sharper.

HORSE-SENSE A degree of wisdom that keeps one from betting on the races.

HOSE Man's excuse for wetting the walk.

HOSIERY Woman's excuse for walking in the wet.

HOTEL A place where a guest often gives up good dollars for poor quarters.

HOUSECLEANING A domestic upheaval that makes it easy for the government to enlist all the soldiers it needs.

HUG A roundabout way of expressing affection.

HUMOR An outbreak, either of skin or brains frequently branded as Rash.

HUNGER Ability to eat in a Night Lunch Cart.

HUSBAND The next thing to a wife. From Eng. *hussy*, woman, and *bond*, tie. Tied to a woman.

HYDRANT From Grk. *hudros*, water, and Eng. *ante*, to give up. Something that gives up water. (A good synonym for Dipsomaniac.)

HYPOCRITE A horse dealer. From Grk. *hippos*, horse, and *kroteo*, to beat. One who beats you on a horse trade.

Home is where the mortgage is.

Aim at a chorus-girl and you may hit a star. —
Stage-Door Secrets.

ICE A substance frequently associated with a tumble in winter, a tumbler in summer, and a skate the year around.

ICEMAN A cool proposition who has Axe-cess to the best families, makes his Weigh in every home and can take his Pick in the kitchen, if he leaves his Chips in the street. "How'd You Like to be The Iceman?"

IDIOT From Eng. *idea*, and *out*. One who is just out of ideas.

IDLE Useless.

IDOLIZE To make useless.

IMPECUNIOUS To be in a state of poverty. From Eng. *in*, and Lat. *pecco*, to sin, poverty being the greatest of all sins.

IMPERIOUS From Eng. *imp*, devil and *aerial*, airy. Airy as the devil.

INCANDESCENT LIGHT

 From Lat. *incendo,* to burn, and Eng. *cent*, meaning money.

An invention for burning money.

INCOME The reliable offspring of a wise investment. From Lat. *in* and *coma*, meaning sleep. Money which works while you sleep.

INDEPENDENCE Self government. Good enough for a Cuban, but too good for a Filipino.

INDIGESTION A distressing stomach trouble that is sometimes temporarily relieved by kicking the cat or whipping the children.

INDIVIDUALITY A harmless trait possessed by one's self. The same trait in others is downright idiocy.

INDORSE To write on the back of; the best indorsed man in town being the Sandwich-Man.

INFANT A disturber of the peace.
INFANTRY A defender of the peace.

INHABITANT A native of any village, town or city. **OLDEST INHABITANT** The Champion Liar.

INTUITION A fictitious quality in females — really Suspicion.

IRRITANT Something which irritates. COUN-
TER IRRITANT A woman shopping.

ISLAND A place where the bottom of the sea
sticks up through the water.

ISOLATION From Eng. *ice,* meaning cold, and
Lat. *solus*, alone. Alone in the cold.

After dinner sit a while, after supper walk a mile—
    And every meal's a supper to the Hobo.

Lies have no legs — That's why we all have to
    stand for them.

JACK An instrument requiring a strong arm, and used for raising heavy weights, or for pulling off the boots.

JACK-POT An instrument requiring a strong hand, and used for raising heavy bets, or for pulling off the stakes.

JAG From the Spanish word *zaga,* meaning a load packed on the outside of a van. In America the load is packed on the inside of a man.

JAM

A pantry composition in A minor.

JANITOR From *jangle,* to quarrel, and *torrid,* meaning hot. Hot and quarrelsome.

JELLY-CAKE Synonym for Belly-Ache.

JERSEY Well knit.
NEW JERSEY Well bit. (See Mosquito).

 **JEW'S HARP** From Jew, a Hebrew, and Harp, a musical instrument, the Jew's musical instrument being a " Sell low ! " (Old spelling, Cello)

JIMMY An implement employed by men of acquisitive natures who cannot afford seats in the Stock Exchange.

JOB An uncertain commodity regulated by a Union Card.

JOCKEY From *jog,* to move slowly, and *key,* something that makes fast. Hence, one who makes the pace fast or slow, according to instructions.

JOINT Either a low limb from the butcher, or a low quarter in town; in either case, the lower the tougher.

JOKE A form of humor enjoyed by some and misunderstood by most; in England, requiring a diagram, raised letters and a club.

JOLLY v. t., To " con " or " josh."

JOLLY BOAT The Ship of State.

JUDGE One who sits on a bench in a court, frames sentences and finishes crooks for a living, and swears continually.

JULEP An insidious friend from the South, who hands you a mint and gives you a sweet spirit, followed shortly by a Bun.

JURY Twelve men chosen to decide who has the better lawyer.

JUSTICE Fair play; often sought, but seldom discovered, in company with Law.

A chip of the old block — A daughter of the
Tenderloin.

One man's meat is another man's finish — Canned
Beef in Cuba.

KANGAROO A hard drinker from Australia, especially fond of hops, and generally carrying a load.

KATYDID A gossiping grasshopper who is always meddling in Katy's affairs.

KEEPSAKE Something given us by someone we've forgotten.

KERNELS or COLONELS Articles often found in cores (or corps) and frequently surrounded by shells.

KEROSENE

An alleged provider of heat and light. From Lat. *carus*, meaning expensive and *seneo*, to be weak; expensive but weak. For further explanation, consult Standard Oil Company.

KEYHOLE

A frequent test for sobriety.

KID Either a boxing-glove or a first-born. In either case, hard to handle until well tanned.

KILTS A Scotchman's apology for indecent exposure.

KINDRED From Eng. *kin,* meaning relation, and *dread*, meaning fear; fearful relations.

KINDERGARTEN From Ger. *kinder*, children, and Lat. *garritus*, a babbling. A place for babbling children.

KINDLING-WOOD From Ger. *kind,* youth, and Eng. *linger,* to loaf. A place where youth generally loafs.

KISS Nothing, divided by two ; meaning persecution for the infant, ecstacy for the youth, fidelity for the middle-aged and homage for the old.

KISS An indescribable something that is of no value to any one but is much prized by the right two.

KNOCKER A device on doors for rousing people ; also, a device on foot for the same purpose.

Laugh-in-one's-sleeve — The direct route to the Funny-Bone.

Two heads are better than one — particularly on a Barrel of Money.

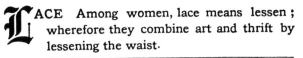**ACE** Among women, lace means lessen ; wherefore they combine art and thrift by lessening the waist.

LACONIC Shy on words. From Eng. *lack,* meaning want, and *connection;* want of connection.

LAMP A light.
LAMPOONED To be lighted on.

LARD Fat.
LARDER A fattener.

LARK A short, sweet spree enjoyed by night hawks. Also, an early rising singing-bird. (Dist. bet. "out on a lark," and "up with the lark," an impossible combination.)

LASSIE One of the weaker sex.
LASSITUDE Slightly weaker.

LAUD Praise for the Almighty.
LAUDANUM Prays for himself — after taking.

LAUNDRY A place where clothes are mangled.

LAUGH A peculiar contortion of the human countenance, voluntary or involuntary, superinduced by a concatenation of external circumstances, seen or heard, of a ridiculous, ludicrous, jocose, mirthful, funny, facetious or fanciful nature and accompanied by a cackle, chuckle, chortle, cachinnation, giggle, gurgle, guffaw or roar.

LAWYER One who defends your estate against an enemy, in order to appropriate it to himself.

LECTURE An entertainment at which it costs but little to look intelligent.

LEGISLATURE

From Lat. *lego,* to bring together, and *latro,* to bark or bluster ; possibly from *lex,* law, and *latens,* unknown. Hence, a company of men brought together to bluster, or a company of law makers who know nothing about law.

LEISURE From Eng, *lazy,* and *sure;* assured laziness.

LENT A Church fast that is slow to go ; or something loaned which is slow to come back.

LIE A very poor substitute for the truth but the only one discovered up to date.

LIMBURGER A native of Germany strong enough to do housework ; well recommended for cleaning out the dining-room.

LIBRARY From Fr. *libre,* meaning free, and proper name ANDY. Something free from Andy Carnegie.

LINKS Found in sausages and golf courses, and both full of hazards.

LION A cruel beast who never patronizes the barber and is always bearded in his den, yet will furnish a close shave if you get near enough.

LOBSTER The edible lobster is found off the New England Coast. The two-legged species is found everywhere. All kinds are green, but when roasted turn a bright red. Soubrettes are very dependent on both varieties for a living ; together they furnish her with food, raiment, flats, diamonds, and occasionally indigestion.

LOBSTER-NEWBURG A dish ordered at hotels by those who usually get beans at home.

LOVE A man's insane desire to become a woman's meal-ticket.

LOVER An ardent admirer who says, " Yes, dearest, I will shovel the snow off the lake so that we can go skating !" and, after marriage remarks, " What ! Shovel the snow off the walk for you ? Well, I should say not ! I'm no chore boy."

Hell is paved with good intentions — also asbestos.

A fool and his wife are soon parted.
    See Alimony.

AGAZINE A receptacle for explosives, literary or mechanical.

MAGNATE One who can float capital in a considerable body of water. From Lat. *magnus*, great, and *nator*, to swim; a great swimmer.

MAIDEN LADY A term applied to an old maid by those who wish to avoid hurting her feelings.

MALT A humble grain which often gets into a ferment, cools off and becomes Stout in its old age.

MAN Something that " Goes first on four feet, then two feet, then three, but the more feet it goes on the weaker it be !"

MAN-ABOUT-TOWN One who is on speaking terms with the head waiter.

MANICURE The only woman who can beat a carpenter at soaking nails.

MANNERS A difficult symphony in the key of B natural.

MARK In Germany, twenty-three cents. In the United States, only Twain.

MASCULINE From Grk. *maskos*, girl, and *eukolos,* easy. Easy for the girls.

MASSAGE A touch, with intent to rub it in.

MATRIMONY A game for women, in which the unmarried half are trying to find a husband and the married half trying not to be found out by one. Both halves are eminently successful.

MEAL According to the Liquor Law, a minute bunch of crumbs entirely surrounded by booze.

MEDIUM A party with one ear in the grave but both hands on your wallet. "Hello, Central! Give me Heaven!"

MELODEON An alleged musical instrument, popular at home, but unpopular next door. From Eng. *melody,* and Latin, *un,* without. Warranted without melody.

MENAGERIE From Fr. *melange,* mixture, and Ger. *riechen,* to smell. A mixture of smells.

MESSENGER BOY From Eng. *miss,* to fail, and Lat. *engeo,* to arrive. One who fails to arrive.

METER The gas man's trysting place. "Meet her in the cellar!"

MIND No matter. **MATTER** Never mind.

MINE A hole in the ground owned by a liar.

MINSTREL A footlight foul that makes its nightly lay in every city.

MIRACLE A woman who won't talk.

MIST Generally, a small, light rain. **SCOTCH MIST** A cloudburst.

MITTEN Something a tender-hearted girl gives a young man when she knows she is going to make it chilly for him.

MONEY Society's vindication of vulgarity.

MONOPOLY A modern device for impoverishing others. From Grk. *monux,* swift-footed, and *polloi,* the people. A swift kick for the people.

MOON The only lighting monopoly that never made money.

MORTGAGE From Fr. *mort,* death, and Eng. *gag,* to choke. A lawyer's invention for choking property to death.

MOSQUITO A small insect designed by God to make us think better of flies.

MOTH An unfortunate acquaintance who is always in the hole. And the only ones who try to get him out are his enemies.

MOUSE

The frequent cause of a rise in cotton.

All gone to 6's and 7's — Ladies' Footwear in
  Chicago.

Time and tide wait for no man — But time always
  stands still for a woman of thirty.

NATURE The author of "The Seasons," an interesting work over which 'Spring pours, Summer smiles, and Autumn turns the leaves while Winter catches the drift of it all.

NECK A close connection between chin and chest, used for the display of linen, silk, furs, jewelry and skin, fitted with gullet, windpipe, hunger and thirst, and devoted to the rubber industry.

NEIGHBOR One who knows more about your affairs than yourself.

NERVE

Breaking the hair-brush on the disobedient scion, then making him pay for a new one. See revised version, "Spare the rod and spoil the hair-brush !"

"NEXT" The barberous password to the heaven of the shaved and the unshaved.

NIP Something bracing from without or within. When felt in the air, it's a frost. When found in a glass, a life saver.

NOBILITY A gang of foreign brigands having abducent designs on the American Damsel and the American Dollar.

NON-CONDUCTOR The motorman.

NOSE A prominent member of the face family, usually a Greek or Roman, who owns the shortest bridge in the world. He is often stuck up in company, but frequently blows himself when he has his grippe. Principal occupations, sniffling, snivelling, sneezing, snorting and scenting, intruding in the neighbors' affairs, stuffing himself without permission and bleeding for others.

NOTE (PROMISSORY) "The substance of things long hoped for, the evidence of things not seen."

NOVEL A fabric that is often (k)nit in print, though the yarn be well spun.

NURSE

One who keeps setting up the drinks after you're all in.

Out of the frying-pan into the face — Mothers' doughnuts.

Many hands make light work — also a good Jack-pot.

OAR A popular device for catching crabs.

OATS England's horse-feed, America's breakfast and Scotland's table-d'hote.

OATH A form of speech that has many trials in court, but is never tried in Sunday School.

OBESITY

A surplus gone to waist.

OCEAN An old toper who is always soaked, has many a hard night along the coast, floats many a schooner, lashes himself into a fury because so frequently crossed, and has his barks in every port. At sea, the king of the elements ; on shore, a mere surf.

OLEOMARGARINE The White Bread's Burden. From Eng. *olio,* a mixture, and Grk. *margino,* to be furious. A furious mixture.

OMNIBUS A test for Patience, still popular in England. From Grk. *oneiros*, dream, and *baino,* to go or move. A dream of motion.

ONION The all-round strength champion of the Vegetable Kingdom, garlic and cabbage being close rivals.

OPERA A drama that has taken on airs and refuses to speak, yet always sings its own praises. **GRAND OPERA** An excuse for displaying several boxes of jewelry and peaches with pedigrees.

OPINION The prodigal son of Thought. **PUBLIC OPINION** The world's champion pugilist, who has knocked out Law in many a hard fought bout.

OPIUM The real author of " The Dream Book."

OPTIMISM A cheerful frame of mind that enables a tea kettle to sing though in hot water up to its nose.

ORCHARD The small boy's Eden of today, in which the apple again occasions the fall.

OSTRICH The largest and heaviest bird on earth, yet rated by his owners only as a featherweight.

OUTSKIRTS The only garments which clothe many a metropolis with decency.

OVEN The only sport who enjoys an equally hot time with or without the dough.

Handsome is what hansoms charge.

Soap, long deferred, maketh the dirt stick.

AIN A sensation experienced on receiving a Punch, particularly the London one.

PALMISTRY A plausible excuse for holding hands.

PANTS Trousers' Country Cousins.

PARACHUTE

A successful method for getting the drop

on the Earth.

PARAGON The model man a woman regrets she gave up for the one she mistakenly married.

PARENTS One of the hardships of a minor's life.

PASS A form of transportation issued free to those who are quite able to pay.

PASSENGER One who does not travel on a pass. (Antonym for Deadhead). From Eng. *pass*, to go, and Grk. *endidomi*, to give up. One who has to give up to go.

PARROT An individual who can never be held responsible for what he says.

PASTRY A deadly weapon carried by cafes, cooks and newly married housekeepers.

PATRIOT One who is willing to take all of Uncle Sam's bonds in a lump.

PAWN

 v. t., To keep property in the family by leaving it all with your Uncle.

PAWNBROKER A mercenary man to whom money is the one redeeming quality.

PEACE A mythical condition of tranquillity frequently reported from the Phillipines.

PEACH A popular synonym for Fair Woman, probably because the peach is largely a skin and stony at heart.

PEARL A small round product manufactured by an oyster, bought by a lobster and worn by a butterfly.

PENITENT From *pen*, meaning to write, and *intent*, meaning determination. One who determines for the right.

PESSIMIST One who paints thing blue. And sometimes red.

PHILISTINE In Bible times, one who worried the children of Israel; today, one who worries only himself. From Grk. *phloios*, bark, and *tino*, to punish. One who barks to punish.

PHILANTHROPIST One who returns to the people publicly a small percentage of the wealth he steals from them privately.

PHILOSPHER One who instead of crying over spilt milk consoles himself with the thought that it was over four-fifths water.

PHILOSOPHY Something that enables the rich to say there is no disgrace in being poor.

PIANO A tool frequently used in building a Rough House.

PIN The best dresser in a woman's acquaintance of remarkable penetration and true as steel, seldom loses its head, follows its own bent and carries its point in whatever it undertakes.

PING-PONG A game invented for the benefit of furniture and crockery dealers.

PITY An emotion awakened in a man's mind when he beholds the children of a woman who might have married him instead.

PLATONIC LOVE An arrangement in which a man and woman attempt a correct imitation of a pair of icicles — and never succeed.

PLENTY A desirable condition that is likely to step out whenever Extravagance steps in.

PLUM A fruit that ripens and falls from the Political Tree — but only after careful grafting.

PLUMB To ascertain the capacity of.

PLUMBER One who ascertians the capacity of your purse, soaks you with a piece of lead and gets away with the money — a process vulgarly known as "a lead-pipe cinch."

POLE-CAT A small animal to be killed with a pole, the longer the pole the better.

POLICEMAN

 A never present help in time of trouble.

POLYGAMY A thoughtless way of increasing the family expenses.

POLYGLOT A parrot that can swear in several languages.

POSTSCRIPT The only thing readable in a woman's letter.

PRETZEL The bar-keeper's promoter.

PROTECTION Originally, the swaddling clothes of the infant, Industry ; now, merely the shoe-lacings for the giant, Monopoly.

PRO and CON Prefixes of opposite meaning. For example, Progress and Congress.

PRUDE A native of Boston.

PRUDENCE A quality of mind that restrains the wise boarder from trying to find out how his landlady makes her hash.

PRUDERY A quality that displays a lack of modesty as a wig does a loss of hair.

PRUNE A plum that has seen better days : the boarding-house veteran and the landlady's pet ; badly wrinkled, yet well preserved.

PUGILIST A close-fisted party who is often roped in but never gives up till he's out.

PULLMAN PORTER A legalized train-robber.

PUNCH A weekly obituary notice from London, chronicling the death of Humor.

Never make a mountain out of a mole-hill — Try gold, silver, copper or radium — there's more in it.

Charity begins at home — but ends when you reach The Cook.

QUACK The Duck family's favorite physician.

QUAIL

 v. t., To shrink — a characteristic of the bird when ordered in a restaurant.

QUEEN One entitled to rule a nation, make up a deck, or beat a knave.

QUESTION Is marriage a failure?

QUEUE The only Mongolian line connecting America and China.

QUORUM A clumsy individual, all Ayes and Noes, who is seldom on hand when needed.

Faint heart never won fair lady — but a full purse
  can always pull the trick.

Man proposes, then woman imposes.

RABBIT   A small rodent, very similar to a hare, which feeds on grass and burrows in the earth.   WELSH RABBIT More like a string, thrives on cheese and burrows in the stomach.

RACE-TRACK   An interesting locality, where pools are bought and sold in books and the heat never interferes with the search for the Pole.

RADIUM   A radiant radiator, redolent of ranging radial rays of radio-activity, raised to radical rates and regarded as a ruthless rake-off in the reign of riches within the arrayed radius of a raging, raving and raided race.

RAG-TIME   Music pulled into many pieces — the invention of a flannel-mouth to which many have cottoned.

RAPID TRANSIT   A municipal myth, circulated for the amusement of the long suffering — and slow moving — public.

THE FOOLISH DICTIONARY.

REFORM In general, a periodic epidemic, starting with marked heat, followed by a high fever, and accompanied by a flow of ink in the newspapers, a discharge of words from the face and a rush of blood to the polls, leaving the victim a chronic invalid until the next campaign. In New York, reform has been confined to a Low attempt at government.

REFORMER One who, when he smells a rat, is eager to let the cat out of the bag.

REGISTER

The only autograph album which it costs you money to write in.

REGRETS An excuse for non-attendance at a social function. Occasionally, an expression of sorrow ; usually, a paean of praise at deliverance from evil.

RELATIONS A tedious pack of people who haven't the remotest knowledge of how to live nor the smallest instinct about when to die.

RELIGION A cloak used by some persons in this world who will be warm enough without one in the next.

R. E. MORSE A veteran General who commands the largest army in the world.

REPARTEE The sassy habit of talking back.

REPUTATION A personal possession, frequently not discovered until lost.

RESIDENCE A rural locality inhabited annually — for a few hours — by a rich New Yorker or Bostonian.

RESOLUTION A fragile bit of crockery fashioned on the first day of January and usually broken on the second.

RESORT (SUMMER) A place where the tired grow more tired. From Eng. *rest*, and Grk. *oriƺo*, to limit. A place where rest is limited.

REST A trade in which every hobo holds a Union Card for life.

RESTAURANT An institution for the spread of dyspepsia. From Lat. *restauro,* to repair, and Grk. *anti,* against. After patronizing, you're "up against repairs."

RHETORIC Language in a dress suit.

RICE An effective field-piece, used for assaulting Chinamen or the newly-married.

ROQUEFORT A kind of cheese whose odor puts it easily in the first rank.

ROYCROFTER A successful book-maker on the East Aurora turf. From Fr. *roi*, king, and old Saxon *crofter,* or grafter. King of Grafters.

RUMOR The long-distance champion of the Human Race — a monster with more tales than an octopus.

RUST Physical dullness.

RUSTIC Mental dullness.

Beggars should never be choosers — though the beggar often chews what he begs.

A miss is as good as her smile,

ADDUCEE A person holding skeptical religous views. Hopeless, hence sad you see.

SAILOR A man who makes his living on water but never touches it on shore.

SANDWICH An unsuccessful attempt to make both ends meat.

SAUSAGE An aftermath of the dog-days.

SCAFFOLD A work of art that rarely fails to get a hanging.

SCARECROW An operator who repeatedly corners corn, without caws.

SCORCHER A chauffeur in an all-fired hurry.

SCULPTOR A poor unfortunate who makes faces and busts.

SELF-MADE Complimentary term for a respectable crook.

SHAMROCK A three-time loser as a racer at sea, but a four-time winner as an " ad." for tea — and Sir T.

SHEPHERD One who depends on a crook for a living.

SHIRT Every man's bosom friend.

SILVER A metallic form of opium, smoked by Presidential impossibilities.

SINNER A stupid person who gets found out.

SNAP A brisk, energetic quality that enables a man with ginger to take the cake.

SNORE An unfavorable report from headquarters.

SOROSIS A female gas company that lays its pipes on cultivated grounds.

SPAGHETTI A table-dish eaten only by Italians and jugglers. From Lat. *spadix,* branch, or fork, and *gestamen,* burden. A burden for the fork.

SPIDER A busy weaver and a good correspondent, who drops a line by every post.

STARS The greatest astronomers known, having studded the heavens for ages.

STAYS A sort of straight-jacket employed in reforming women.

STOCKINGS Woman's only savings for A Rainy Day.

STOCKS An unreliable commodity bought and sold by gamblers. If you win, it's an investment ; if you lose, a speculation.

STOVE-PIPE

 A movable cylinder used as a receptacle for smoke and profanity.

SPRING Formerly a very delightful season but now obsolete except in poetry and the Old Farmer's Almanac.

SPINSTER An ember from which the sparks have flown.

SUBWAY In Boston, a place where one may enjoy continuous disturbance of the peace, disorderly conduct, assault and battery, riot and rebellion. These events are allowed by law, and the entry-fee is five cents.

SUCCESS A goal usually reached by those who employ their time in cultivating a more definite aim in life rather than in searching for a larger target.

SUMMER An oppressive and expensive season invented by rural cottage and hotel owners, railroad and steamboat companies and the Iceman.

SUN A yellow arrival from Way Down East who goes west daily, operates a heating and lighting trust, draws water, prints pictures, developes crops, liquidates the ice business and tans skins on the side. Profits by his daily rays and always has a shine.

SYMPATHY

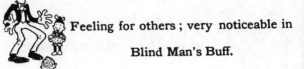

Feeling for others ; very noticeable in Blind Man's Buff.

SYNDICATE A conspiracy to extend the modest business established by Captain Kidd.

Fortune knocks only once at a man's door — And she's the worst Knocker in the world.

Brevity is the soul of wit — and the sole charm of of a bicycle-skirt.

TAILOR One who takes your measure on first sight, gives you a fit, sews you up and follows suit until paid.

TALK A continuous performance playing daily and nightly engagements, with Woman as the star and Man confined in the Family Circle.

TELEGRAM

A form of correspondence sent by a man in a hurry and carried by a boy in sleep.

TELEPHONE From Eng. *tell*, to talk, and Grk. *phonos*, murder. A machine in which talk is murdered.

TENNIS A game in which the participants enjoy a racket on the side and raise the deuce over a net, while the volleys drive them from set to set and love scores as often as it's mentioned.

TEMPER A quality, the loss of which is likely to make a knife blade dull and a woman's tongue sharp.

THERMOMETER

A short, glass tube that regulates the weather — and usually does a poor job.

THIRST A sensation immediately following a short session at the free lunch stand.

TIDE An old friend who comes and goes daily but is all in whenever he gets over the bay.

TITIAN The color a poor red-headed girl's hair becomes as soon as her father strikes oil.

TIPS Wages we pay other people's hired help.

TOBACCO A nauseating plant that is consumed by but two creatures; a large, green worm and — man. The worm doesn't know any better.

TONGUE An unruly member that is frequently put out, yet an artist who's a hard worker at the palate and a great wag among women.

TOUCH A habit common to the impecunious, causing in its victim a feeling of faintness, followed by a chill or a sense of loss.

TRANSFER A small bit of paper of remarkable strength, being able to carry a heavy man several miles.

TROLLEY-CAR A conveyance filled with advertisements, and occasionally passengers, and operated by Poles.

TROUBLE Something that many are looking for but no one wants.

TRUST A small body of capital entirely surrounded by water.

TWINS Insult added to Injury.

TWISTERS

 An undesirable thing to have on hand.

It's a wise son who can get two birds with One Bone.

There is a tide in the affairs of men, which, taken at the flood, leads on to Fortune — But most of us catch our watered stock on the ebb.

UMBRELLA A good thing to put up in a shower—or pawn-shop; but, like skating, never seen after Lent.

UNBOSOMED

A shirt just returned from a steam laundry.

UNION An ailing individual frequently troubled by scabs and liable to strike without warning.

UMPIRE No jeweler, but a high authority on diamonds.

USHER One who takes a leading part in a theatre.

VACCINATION Where "jabbing the needle" is never a vice.

VAUDEVILLE From Lat· *vaut*, good for, and *villageois*, countryman. Good for countrymen.

VERANDA

An open-air enclosure often used as a spoon-holder.

VEST A waistcoat sold at halfprice.

VIRTUE A quality oftentimes associated with intelligence, but rarely with beauty.

VULGARITY The conduct of others.

A rolling stone gathers no moss — except at roulette.

But a stony roll always gathers the stony stare.

WAITER   An Inn-experienced servant.

WAR   A wholesale means of making heroes which, if planned in a small way, would produce only murderers.

WATER   A thin substance applied to stocks with which to soak buyers.

WEDDING   A trade in which the bride is generally given away, and the groom is often sold.

WEEDS   Found in gardens and widows.   For removing easily, marry the widow.

WICKEDNESS   A myth invented by good people to account for the singular attractiveness of others.

WIDOW   The wife of a golfer during the open season, unless she golfs, too.   In that event the children are golf orphans.

WHISKY Trouble put up in liquid form.

WIND An aerial phenomenon, superinduced by an ephemeral agitation of the nebular strata, whereby air, (hot or cold), impelled into transitory activity, generates a prolonged passage through space, owing to certain occult ethereal stimuli, and results in zephyrs, breezes, blows, blow-outs, blizzards, gales, simoons, hurricanes, tornadoes or typhoons. Barred from Kansas Cyclone-cellars but frequently blended with Chicago tongue — canned or conversational.

WOMAN An aspiring creature whose political sphere is still slightly flattened at the polls.

WORD Something you must keep after giving it to another.

WORRY A state of mind that leads some persons to fear, every time the tide goes out, that it won't come in again.

WRINKLES A merchant's trade-marks.

It's the first straw hat which shows how the
wind blows.

A Ride goeth before a Fall.—
See Automobile, Bucking Broncho, Bicycle, Air-
Ship, Patrol-Wagon, Rail, and Go-Cart.

X RAYS

Ten dollars from a friend.

YARN   An essential in fabrication — either woven or narrated. Mill yarns are highly colored; those spun at sea much more so.

YAWL   Either the shape of a boat or the sound of a cat, but never a cat-boat.

YAWNS   The air-breaks on a sleeper.

YEAR   A period originally including 365 days, now 325, since the other 40 are Lent.

YELLOW FEVER   A passion for reading the Hearst newspapers.

YOLK The legacy of the hen and the burden of its lay.

YOKE The inheritance of the hen-pecked and the burden of the married.

YULE-LOG A Christmas protege of the grate, too young to smoke, too tough to burn and too green to warm up to anybody.

YOUTH The dynamo that makes the world go round; a product of its own generation, with its wires carrying Power into the high places of Earth and with its currents of Thought short-circuited only by bigoted Old Age.

ZEALOT One who loves morality so well he will commit crime to maintain it.

ZEBRA The crook among horses, condemned to wear stripes for life.

ZERO Originally, nothing; but now meaning a good deal on a thermometer or bank-draft, and comprising two-thirds of the 400.

ZIGZAG The popular route after a heavy dinner. Old adage, " The longest way round is the drunkard's way home !"

ZOUAVE

The original Mrs. Bloomer.

Postage and Postal Information.

How to Mail a Letter.

After writing it, place it in a square or oblong envelope—round ones are no longer fashionable—seal it on the back and write a legible address on the front; then take a two-cent stamp, give it a good licking and retire it to the corner — the upper, right-hand corner, on the outside—never inside, as the postmaster is not a clairvoyant. Drop it in a letter-box and trust to luck. If it's a love letter, it will probably reach her all right, for Cupid is a faithful postman and carries a stout pair of wings. If it's a bill, by all means have it registered; otherwise, your debtor will swear he never got it. If it's cash for your tailor, heed the post-office warning, "Don't send money through the mails." Wait until you happen to meet him on the street. If he sees you first, you lose.

First-class Matter.

Anything you are ashamed to have the postmaster or postmistress read, and therefore seal up, is known as first-class matter. Also, postal cards, where you're only allowed to argue on one side. If you think your letter should travel slowly, invest ten cents in a Special Delivery Stamp. This will insure a nice, leisurely journey, lasting from one to two days longer than by the cheap two-cent route.

Second-class Matter.

This class was originated for the benefit of Patent Medicine Mixers, who print circulars on "What Ails You" four times a year, and pepper the land with "Before-and-after-taking" caricatures, at the rate of one cent a pound.

Third-class Matter.

While the quack nostrums travel second-class for one cent a pound, books, engravings, manuscript copy, and works of art have to go third-class and are taxed one cent for every two ounces. They must also be left open for inspection, thus affording the post-office employee a fleeting acquaintance with something really useful.

Fourth-class Matter.

Everything not included in the above, except poisons, explosives, live animals, insects, inflammable articles, and things giving off a bad odor. The last two do not include *The Police Gazette* or *The Philistine*.

A Few Mythological and Classical Names

Brought down to date in brief Notes by the Editor.

ACHILLES. A courageous Greek, who did a general slaughtering business in Troy in 1180 B.C., but was finally pinked in the heel — his only vulnerable spot — and died.

Long life often depends on being well heeled.

ADONIS. A beautiful youth, beloved by Venus and killed by a boar.

———

Bores have been the death of us ever since.

———

BACCHUS. A brewer, who supplied the Gods with nectar, the beer that made Olympus famous.

———

Those desiring a drink, please ask Dickens if " Bacchus is willin'."

———

CASTOR AND POLLOX. Two clever sports and twin brothers from Greece, Castor being a horse-trainer and Pollux a pugilist, whose sister, Helen, a respectable, married woman, disgraced the family by eloping with Paris.

———

Just because a man can break a broncho or win a prize fight, it's no sign he can manage a woman.

CERBERUS. A dog with three heads, a serpent's tail and several snakes around his neck, who guarded the main entrance to Hades.

———

When a man begins to see snakes and one head looks like three, it's a cinch he's not far from Hell.

CHARON. The gloomy gondolier of the Styx, who carried the dead to the Other World—if they paid him first.

———

And even to-day, he who patronizes Rapid Transit must pay his fare in advance.

CUPID. The son of Venus and the God of Love, who with bow and arrows punctured men's bosoms with the darts of admiration.

———

But now-a-days the arrow's not in it with a snug bathing suit or a decollette gown.

DAEDALUS. The original Santos Dumont, who invented and successfully operated a flying-machine that would fly. His son, Icarus, tried the trick, went too high and fell into the sea.

A flier frequently precedes a fall — especially in Wall Street.

DIANA. The goddess of the chase; unmarried.

And this is very fitting. May the chase always be for the unmarried only!

HERCULES. The Gritty Greek (no relation to the Terrible Turk), an independent laborer, who always had a good job awaiting him.

It is interesting to recall the days when non-union labor had all the work it wanted.

IXION. A king of Thessaly, who for his sins was broken on a wheel.

And men have been going broke on "the wheel" ever since.

LOTUS EATERS. A gang of ancient vegetarians, who chewed leaves and went to sleep.

Now succeeded by a club of New Yorkers, who chew the rag and keep awake.

MERCURY. A celestial messenger-boy, who wore wings on his shoes and knew how "to get there" in a hurry.

Now they all wear hobbles, and never exceed the speed limit in a public thoroughfare.

MIDAS. A Greek king, who had the power of turning into gold all that he touched.

That's nothing! There are plenty of men to-day who always get gold whoever they touch.

SAPPHO. A love-lorn poetess, who, failing to win the man she first loved, cured herself by jumping into the Mediterranean.

She probably acted on the old advice, "There's plenty more fish in the sea!"

TANTALUS. A proud king, who suffered in Hades the agonies of hunger and thirst, with food and drink always in sight, but always beyond reach.

Here on earth, the 50-cent table d'hote accomplishes the same result — besides costing you the fifty.

TROY. An ancient, oriental city, which took in a wooden horse and saw the domestic finish of Helen and Paris.

Do not confuse with Troy, N. Y., where they only take in washing and provide a domestic finish for collars and shirts.

VULCAN. The Olympian blacksmith, who always had his hammer with him

---

But not all who carry hammers are blacksmiths.

Legal and Local Holidays in the United States.

JANUARY 1, New Year's Day. On this day the Flowing Bowl is filled — and emptied — and the Genial Palm circulated in forty-three States and Territories out of forty-nine. In Massachusetts, New Hampshire, Rhode Island, Arkansas, Oklahoma and the Indian Territory there is no celebration. The natives are too busy collecting good resolutions and bad bills.

FEBRUARY 22, Washington's Birthday.
(George, not Booker), is remembered by
thirty-eight of the States. On this day,
in the public schools, are shown pictures
of George Chopping the Cherry Tree
and Breaking Up the Delaware Ice Trust,
Valley Forge in Winter, and Mt. Vernon
on a Busy Day. The Pride of the Class
recites Washington's "Farewell to the
Army," Minnie the Spieler belabors the
piano with the "Washington Post
March," and the scholars all eat Washington Pie, made of "Columbia, the Jam
of the Ocean."

**MARCH 17, St. Patrick's Day and Evac-
uation Day,** when the British redcoats got
out of Boston and Patrick evicted the
snakes from Ireland. For observing the
day, wear a turkey-red coat, or vest, and
put a bit of green ribbon, or a shamrock,
in the buttonhole — the green above he
red. On Easter day, wear a scrambled
egg in the same place.

APRIL 19, Patriot's Day. A New England successor to FAST DAY — the slowest day of the year. Originally invented for Fasting and Prayer. Now used exclusively for opening the Baseball Season, Locating a Seashore Home for the Summer, and watching Red-Shirted Diogenes at his Tub.

> Little drops of water,
> Little lines of hose,
> Make the mighty Muster
> As ev'ry Laddie knows.

MAY 1, Moving Day. Observed everywhere by The Restless Tenant.

APRIL 26 } **MAY 30** } Memorial Days { In "Dixie" { In the North
A Symphony in Blue and Gray.

JUNE 17, Bunker Hill Day. Celebrated in Boston, Mass., by a procession of the Ancient and Horrible Distillery Company, a few of the City Fathers in hacks, a picked bunch of Navy Yard sailors and occasionally a few samples from a Wild

West Show. For 24 hours, pistols and firecrackers are allowed to mutilate Young America *ad lib*.

JULY 4, Independence Day. A national holiday, invented for the benefit of popcorn and peanut promoters; tin horn and toy-balloon vendors; lemonade chemists; dealers in explosives; physicians and surgeons. A grand chance for the citizen-soldier to hear the roar of battle, smell powder, shoot the neighbor's cat, and lose a night's rest — or a finger.

LABOR DAY, First Monday in September. The only day when labor works overtime. An occasion when the workingman takes a cane in place of a dinner-pail and proudly tramps the streets behind a real silk banner and a Hod Carrier on a Cart Horse.

THANKSGIVING DAY (Last Thursday in November). A day devoted to the annual division of Turkey — with Greece on the side — by the Hung'ry folks.

DECEMBER 25, Christmas Day. Another national holiday, marked by the following observances: Filling the young and helpless with a lot of fiction about Santa Claus, the old chimney fakir, who went up the flue long ago; making a clothesline of the mantelpiece and robbing the forest of its young; swapping several things we'd like to keep for a lot of stuff we don't want; and, finally, putting on in church a Sunday night performance of light opera, known as "The Sabbath School Concert."

LETTERS FROM A SON
TO HIS Self-Made Father

CHARLES EUSTACE MERRIMAN'S WISE
AND WITTY ANSWERS TO "LETTERS
FROM A SELF-MADE MERCHANT TO HIS
SON."

Harry Thurston Peck wrote in the New York
American, February 6:

"Fully as amusing as the book that suggested
it."

ARTISTICALLY BOUND IN CLOTH, GILT TOP,
ILLUSTRATED, $1.25

THE ROBINSON, LUCE COMPANY,
209 WASHINGTON STREET, BOSTON.

MORE FACSIMILE REISSUES FROM PRYOR PUBLICATIONS

MANNERS for MEN

'Like every woman, I have my ideal of manhood. The difficulty is to describe it. First of all, he must be a gentleman; but that means so much that it, in its turn, requires explanation . . .'

£4.50

MANNERS for WOMEN

'A useful reminder that tittering is an unpleasant habit and that curtseying should be avoided unless you know what you are doing.' The Times

£3.95

Don't: A Manual of Mistakes and Improprieties more or less prevalent in Conduct and Speech.

100,000 COPIES SOLD OF OUR EDITION.

£3.50

WHAT SHALL I SAY?

A guide to letter writing for ladies first published in 1898 this book covers everything from complaining of being attacked by a vicious dog to a lover complaining of coldness.

£3.50

Available from bookshops or post free from

PRYOR PUBLICATIONS

75 Dargate Road, Yorkletts, Whitstable, Kent CT5 3AE, England.
Tel. & Fax: (0227) 274655

A full list of our publications sent free on request.